# HiS-STORY

## A WALK THROUGH BIBLE HISTORY
## THROUGH THE EYES OF A CHILD

Renee Bullard

WestBow Press books may be ordered through booksellers or by contacting:

WestBow Press
A Division of Thomas Nelson & Zondervan
1663 Liberty Drive
Bloomington, IN 47403
www.westbowpress.com
844-714-3454

Scripture taken from the HOLY BIBLE: EASY-TO-READ VERSION ©2014 by Bible League International. Used by permission.

ISBN: 978-1-6642-7893-6 (sc)
ISBN: 978-1-6642-7894-3 (e)

Library of Congress Control Number: 2022917849

Print information available on the last page.

WestBow Press rev. date: 05/04/2023

WESTBOW
PRESS®
A DIVISION OF THOMAS NELSON
& ZONDERVAN

Matthew 19:14

But Jesus said, suffer little children and forbid them not, to come unto me for of such is the kingdom of heaven.

This book is dedicated to our father, the late Pastor Fred Bullard. He was an amazing father who taught and instilled the Word of God in his children at an early age.

We are continuing his legacy by planting and instilling the Word of God in the early years of our children, grandchildren, and children all over the world.

Dad, we love you!

4

# HiS-STORY
## CHILDREN'S BOOK
## PRESENTED

**To:**_____

**From:**_____

**Date:**_____

It all started when God saw that the earth was not a good place for mankind to live. It was dark, gloomy, and dirty. One day he decided to clean it up... and with this His-Story begins. God started to clean up the earth to make it look very beautiful. After cleaning the earth and making it beautiful, God gave the earth to the first man and the first woman and all the beautiful animals which he made in six days.

The earth was now man's home, and it was spotless and clean and full of beautiful trees, bushes, and flowers. Man was named Adam and his wife was called woman before Adam named her Eve. They lived on the earth in a garden called Eden.

In this garden, God gave man every fruit, nut, vegetable, and herb that he could eat, EXCEPT one fruit on a certain tree called the Tree of Knowledge that stood in the middle of the garden.

God was testing man and his wife. He told them do not disobey him and do not eat from the tree of knowledge... for when they do, they will no longer live.

God was Man and Woman's friend. He loved them and they loved him. They had a good and blessed friendship.

God gave Adam and his wife control over all the animals, bugs, trees, and flowers. God also told them to have lots of babies, so that they would fill the earth up again with people. While being good by doing what God told them to do, they were also to live blessed lives unto God.

But, one day, the Serpent who also lived in the Garden of Eden, started talking with the Devil! The Serpent was the wisest and the trickiest of all the animals. And the Devil knew this!

So, the Devil decided to talk the Serpent into helping him do evil, by telling a lie to Adam and Eve so they would lose their friendship with God... and it worked!

9

The Serpent through the direction of the Devil tricked Adam and Eve by telling them a lie; that it was ok to eat off the tree God told them not to.

And because they listened to the Serpent and ate from the Tree of Knowledge; man and woman became bad in God's eyes, and so, did the Serpent and all the other animals.

This all happened because the Serpent went along with the Devil's evil plan to break up Adam and Eve's friendship with God. Adam and Eve and all the animals had to leave God's beautiful Garden of Eden; because God is good and clean, and now they were all bad and dirty.

Not only did Adam and the Serpent actions cause all the animals and the people to become bad and dirty, but it also made the earth become dirty again too!

God knew that he had to do something to keep Adam, Eve, and the animals from returning to his clean and beautiful Garden of Eden, so they would not eat from the Tree of Life and stay bad and dirty forever.

So, God placed an angel with a fiery sword at the doorway of the Garden of Eden; to stand and guard it, so that no one and no animal could ever come back again.

But, God missed the friendship he had with Adam and Eve and wanted to be their friend again, but to be their friend, they and all of mankind must be cleaned.

Adam and Eve were now both bad and dirty and were unable to clean themselves the way God needed them to be cleaned.

To make us clean, God had a plan. He knew the only way that man and woman could be clean is if he washed and cleansed them himself. So, God came down in the form of a man named Jesus Christ to clean us. Jesus showed us how to do the things he wanted us to do, and how to live the way he wants us to live.

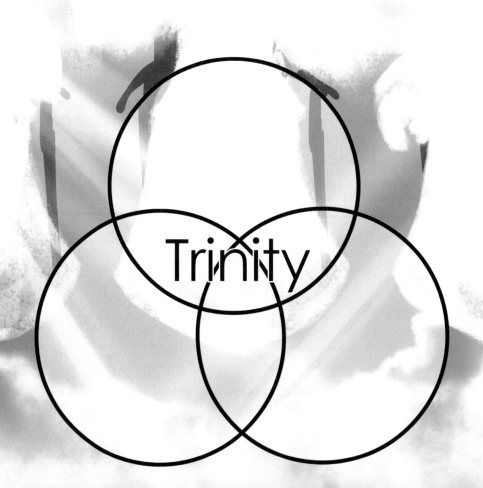

Jesus Christ, the Son of God, showed us that we can live holy (and clean), but to do this, we must accept and believe in him that he is not only God's son but also God, and then we must live the way he told us to live. This will make us clean.

But, everyone didn't like Jesus Christ. They didn't like the way he talked, they didn't like what he had to say, they didn't like how he lived his life, and they didn't like how he was telling men and women (mankind) how they should live theirs.

But, the true reason those people didn't like Jesus was because they were the Devil's children and they only wanted bad things to happen to Jesus; so bad, that they even wanted to take his life.

But, God's plan was to give us eternal life, instead of a punishment of death. Death means, we would be separated from God forever!

Jesus, who is life, said he would take our punishment of death for us, so that we may live. All who believe that Jesus did this for them, he will give them life and let them live with him in heaven forever and ever.

But, the Devil did not know this and planned to have his children take the life of Jesus.

The Devil is so wicked and evil, and he doesn't like God. He hates everything God created, and he wants man to stay dirty and bad with him, so they all could be punished together.

Because the Devil is so bad, his children are also bad, and it shows in the things they do. They planned together of how they could get rid of Jesus.

BUT, because Jesus Christ is God, no one could take his life, but he willingly gave up his life by letting the Devil carry out his plan through his children.

19

Jesus' love is so great, that he took everyone's punishment and suffered on the cross for us all. He gave his life, died on the cross and came back to life three days later.

When Jesus died and came back to life, he told all those who loved him and followed his way of living... to tell everyone they know about him. "After the Lord Jesus said these things to his followers, he was carried up into heaven. There, Jesus sat at the right side of God."

This was the purpose for Jesus dying and coming back to life to give all those who love him and live like he lived, life forever.

We will live forever with Jesus after our time on this earth is done, and Jesus calls us home.

That is why, Jesus is asking everyone to believe and receive him now. He gave up his eternal life in heaven, in exchange for everyone's punishment of eternal death. For we know that one day he is going to come back and get all those who love him and is living life the way he did on earth.

And because we believe what Jesus said, accepted what he has done and welcomed him into our hearts; we now know Jesus and he knows us. And anyone who knows Jesus, also knows God!

Sending Jesus into the world to die for the bad things that we do, so that we could get to know, and accept him as our Lord and Savior was all a part of God's plan, to make us clean again.

If we believe that he died, rose from the dead and show it with our actions by asking him to be our Lord and Savior; we will become God's friend and will have everlasting life.

Since we are his friends, he gives us his Holy Bible to read, so we will know what he wants us to do, and how he wants us to live. This will make us good and stay friends with him forever.

He also places his Holy Spirit in our hearts to live, teach us, and keep us from doing bad things so God would be happy with us. But, God only gives us the Holy Spirit if we believe and accept Jesus as our Lord and Savior.

So, accept Jesus in your hearts today, so you can forever live with him in heaven.

Amen

**Romans 10:9 (ERV)**
If you openly say, "Jesus is Lord" and believe in your heart that God raised him from death, you will be saved.

**II Corinthians 6:2 (ERV)**
God says, "I heard you at the right time, and I gave you help on the day of salvation." I tell you that the "right time" is now. The "day of salvation" is now.

# WORK CITED

Pg 6     Genesis Chp.1 & 2

Pg 7     Genesis Chp.1 & 2

Pg 8     Genesis Chp.2

Pg 9     Genesis Chp.3

Pg 10    Genesis Chp.3

Pg 11    Genesis Chp.3

Pg 12    Genesis Chp.3

Pg 14    John Chp.1; John Chp.3:16

Pg 15    John Chp.3:1-21; John Chp.5: 17-24

Pg 16    John Chp.5; John Chp.10: 22-42

Pg 17    John Chp.3:16

Pg 18    1 John Chp.3:8; John Chp.5:18

Pg 19    John Chp.10:17-18

Pg 20    John Chp.3:16; Mark Chp.16:19; Romans Chp.10:9

Pg 21    John Chp.14:2; Romans Chp.10:9;
             John Chp.3:16; Matthew Chp.24:36,42

Pg 22    John Chp.10:14-18, Romans Chp.10:9

# AUTHOR BIOGRAPHY

She has been a Born Again Believer since the early age of nine years old, and a witness of the Gospel of Jesus Christ throughout her primary, secondary, college educational years and throughout her career. She has successfully raised her three children (from the ages of 4, 2, and 1 to ages 20, 18, and 17) after becoming a widow at an early age. All her children are born again believers, and two of the three children have successfully graduated from two of the top High Schools in Detroit, Michigan with the last child trailing quickly behind his siblings success with a gpa of 3.96 at Cass Technical High School. Her passion for teaching goes beyond her own children. She wants all children to be successful in their learning and go beyond what they believe they are capable of doing. She is very creative in her techniques, when it comes to teaching children the Word of God, from making up songs, to telling stories, to acting out plays. Her desire and goal is to help children understand the word of God, experience his great love and peace, and encourage them to become a part of God's family.

Printed in the United States
by Baker & Taylor Publisher Services